The Cool, Awesome, Simple Science Series

# Hands-On Physical Science

## for Elementary Grades

by

## Phil Parratore

# Table of Contents

© Carson-Dellosa CD-7322

# Accordion

2 minutes

## What You Will Do

Display how water molecules are attracted to one another.

## Get it Together

- ◆ Construction paper
- ◆ Bowl of water

## Procedure

1. Fold a strip of construction paper like an accordion. Each fold should be about 1" wide.
2. Lightly dip one end of your accordion in the water, then carefully place it on top of the water in the bowl.

## A Closer Look

The molecules of water and the paper carry both a positive and negative charge. As you placed the paper in the bowl, it quickly absorbed the water and acted like a magnet that was strong enough to pull the wet end of the paper into the water. The folds simply helped the paper move more easily.

3

© Carson-Dellosa CD-7322

# Water's Great Escape

15 minutes

## What You Will Do

Demonstrate capillary action.

## Get it Together

◆ Glass
◆ Bowl
◆ Paper towels
◆ Water

## Procedure

1. Fill the glass nearly full of water.
2. Set the glass next to the bowl.
3. Twist several paper towels together to form a wick-like shape as shown in the illustration.
4. Bend the wick near the middle.
5. Place one end of the wick in the glass, and the other end in the bowl. Wait 10 minutes.

### A Closer Look

Within a few minutes you notice the wick getting wet as water begins to travel along the towel. After another few minutes some water appears in the bottom of the bowl. There are millions of tiny tube-like fibers in the paper towels. Water moves into these tubes and advances along the twisted material. This movement is known as capillary action. This is one way that moisture moves from plant roots into the rest of the plant.

© Carson-Dellosa CD-7322

## Capillary Action
# You're My Shining Star

5 minutes

## What You Will Do

Illustrate water absorption through capillary action.

## Get it Together

◆ 5 flat toothpicks
◆ Eyedropper
◆ Water

## Procedure

1. Bend each toothpick at the center to form a V-shape.
2. Place the five V-shaped toothpicks on a very smooth surface with the bent sections all meeting in the middle. The arrangement should look like a wagon-wheel.
3. Put 1 drop of water in the center, where all the toothpicks meet.
4. Observe.

### A Closer Look

The toothpicks wiggled around as water was drawn up through the wood fibers. This process, known as capillary action, is the upward movement of water through a tube. It happens because water molecules like to "stick" to the sides of a tube. The water continues to climb until the whole tube is wet. Water molecules also like to "stick" together, so when the first water molecules climb the wood fibers, the rest play "follow the leader."

5

© Carson-Dellosa CD-7322

## Density
# Circle of Oil

5 minutes

## What You Will Do

Display the differences in the densities of alcohol and oil.

## Get it Together

- ◆ Small, clear, glass jar
- ◆ Rubbing alcohol
- ◆ Food coloring
- ◆ Water
- ◆ Small funnel
- ◆ Cooking oil

## Procedure

1. Fill the jar half full with water.
2. Add a few drop of food coloring. Stir.
3. Use the funnel to slowly pour a few spoonfuls of oil into the jar.
4. Add a small amount of rubbing alcohol, and observe how the oily layer "bends" in the center.
5. Continue adding the alcohol until the oily layer becomes a sphere floating in the middle of the liquid.

### A Closer Look

The alcohol, when mixed with the water, makes it less dense. The watery mixture exerts less force against the oily layer, so the oil starts to sink down into the watery mix. As you add more alcohol, the mix starts to "push" on the oil equally from all directions. This makes the oil form a sphere.

### Attention!
Use caution when working with alcohol.

## Clean Up

Flush the liquids down the drain with water. Recycle the glass jar.

© Carson-Dellosa CD-7322

Density

# Color Me Oily

5 minutes

## What You Will Do

Show how oil and water do not mix.

## Get it Together

- 2 white strips of construction paper
- 2 Tbsp. cooking oil
- 2 Tbsp. water
- 2 shallow dishes
- Paper towels
- Food coloring

## A Closer Look

The food coloring, which is made from water, sits on the oiled paper because its water molecules will not combine with the oil molecules. However, the water-based food coloring combines with the water molecules on the other paper and spreads out.

## Procedure

1. Place the oil in one dish and the water in the other.
2. Dip one strip of construction paper into the oil dish and the other strip into the water dish.
3. Lay both strips on the paper towel.
4. Place a drop of food coloring on the dipped portion of each strip.

**Attention!**
Food coloring stains clothing.

## Clean Up

Wash the oil dish with soap and water.

## What Now?

Dip the paper in other liquids and observe the affect on food coloring.

© Carson-Dellosa CD-7322

## Density
# Erupting Colors

5 minutes

## What You Will Do

Show how oil and water do not mix.

## Get it Together

- Clear, glass bowl
- 1 Tbsp. cooking oil
- 3 different colors of food coloring
- Small cup
- Fork
- Water

## Procedure

1. Fill the bowl with water.
2. Pour the oil into the cup and add four drops of each of the food colorings.
3. Use the fork to beat the oil/food coloring until thoroughly mixed.
4. Slowly pour the mixture into the water.

## A Closer Look

Oil and water are considered immiscible materials. This means they do not mix with one another. The water remains in tiny spheres throughout the oil on the water's surface. The round, colored spheres sink through the oil layers and dissolve in the water layer below. At the moment the tiny drops of color touch the water, they quickly flatten on the surface, and long streamers of color begin their descent.

8

© Carson-Dellosa CD-7322

# Float the Boat

## What You Will Do

Demonstrate that boats can float and carry weight.

## Get it Together

- Modeling clay
- Container filled with water
- Peas, dried beans, or other small "weights"

### A Closer Look

The clay is shaped in such a way that it displaces or pushes aside more water than the volume it occupies. As you increase the mass of the boat by adding additional weight, the boat and its cargo become heavier than the water and your boat sinks.

## Procedure

1. Using a small chunk of clay, design any type of boat. Make sure that the center of your boat can hold the small weights.
2. Test to see if your boat floats. If not, remodel it.
3. Once your boat floats, predict how many small weights your boat will hold.
4. Test your boat by adding one weight at a time until it sinks.

© Carson-Dellosa CD-7322

# Heavy Ice

1 minute

## What You Will Do

Demonstrate the differences in density between water and alcohol.

## Get it Together

- ◆ 2 clear glasses
- ◆ 1 cup water
- ◆ 1 cup rubbing alcohol
- ◆ 2 ice cubes

## Procedure

1. Put the water in one glass; the alcohol in the other.
2. Place an ice cube in each.

### A Closer Look

Alcohol is less dense than water and will float to the surface when mixed with water. The ice cube will sink in the alcohol because ice is "heavier," or denser, than alcohol. Ice is also less dense than liquid water so it normally floats on the water's surface.

### Attention!
Use caution when working with alcohol.

## Clean Up

Flush all liquids down the drain with water.

10

© Carson-Dellosa CD-7322

**Density**

# Water and Oil Don't Mix

15 minutes

## What You Will Do

Demonstrate the differences in the densities of ice, oil, and water.

## Get it Together

◆ Clear container
◆ Ice cube
◆ Vegetable or mineral oil

### A Closer Look

Ice is less dense than oil, and oil is less dense than water. In a cup of oil, ice will float on top. However, as the ice melts and becomes water, it becomes more dense than the oil, and so it sinks and settles beneath the oil.

## Procedure

1. Pour oil in the container so that it is $3/4$ full.
2. Float the ice cube in the oil and observe.

## Clean Up

Place oil in a sealed container and put in the trash.

## What Now?

Put oil in a plastic, one-liter soda bottle. Add food coloring if desired. Try floating some other materials in the oil such as alcohol, cork, glycerin, Karo™ syrup, or metal.

© Carson-Dellosa CD-7322

# Cool Cubes

10 minutes

## What You Will Do

Demonstrate that salt affects the freezing point of water.

## Get it Together

- 2 identical, clear glasses
- 4 ice cubes
- 2 thermometers
- 2 Tbsp. salt
- Water
- Spoon

## Procedure

1. Fill the two glasses with water.
2. In one glass, stir in the salt until it dissolves.
3. In each of the glasses, place two ice cubes and a thermometer.
4. Compare the temperatures of the two glasses.

### A Closer Look

Pure water freezes at 32° Fahrenheit. When salt is added to the water, the freezing temperature is lowered. A lower freezing temperature means that more heat stays in the glass with the salt water, causing the ice cubes to melt faster. Salt's fast melting power is why it is used on icy streets in many cold weather climates.

12

© Carson-Dellosa CD-7322

Heat Energy
# Holdin' in the Heat

1 minute+

## What You Will Do

Demonstrate a difference in heat absorption between different colors.

## Get it Together

- 2 white, plastic foam cups
- Black construction paper
- White construction paper
- Tape
- 2 thermometers
- Room temperature water
- Sunny day
- Window ledge

## Procedure

1. Fill both cups about ⅔ full of water.
2. Place a thermometer in each cup.
3. Tape the black construction paper over the mouth of one cup and the white construction paper over the mouth of the other.
4. Place both cups beside a sunny window for about 30 minutes and leave undisturbed. Make sure the sun is directly hitting both cups.
5. Remove the papers from the cups and read the temperatures of each.

### A Closer Look

Dark colors absorb more of the sun's energy than light colors. The light absorbed by the black construction paper is changed to heat and the heat raises the temperature of the water. The white construction paper reflects much of the sun's light, so it is not available to be converted to heat. The cup covered with white construction paper should have a lower temperature.

## What Now?

Allow the containers to sit for 60 minutes, 90 minutes, and 120 minutes. Record the temperatures after each time. Compare. Try different colors of construction paper.

© Carson-Dellosa CD-7322

## Heat Energy
# It Didn't Touch My Lips

5 minutes

## What You Will Do

Demonstrate that heat causes air to expand.

## Get it Together

- ◆ Small glass bottle with a small opening
- ◆ 6" to 8" latex balloon
- ◆ Heat source (i.e. candle, hot water, stove)
- ◆ Oven mitt

## Procedure

1. Stretch the balloon over the neck of the empty bottle.
2. Hold the bottle near the neck and slowly apply heat to the base of the bottle. Observe.

### A Closer Look

When heat is applied to the bottle, the air molecules inside the bottle move faster and get farther apart. This causes the air to expand. As the air takes up more space, it moves into the balloon and pushes against the elastic walls of the balloon, causing it to inflate.

### Attention!

Use caution when using your heat source. Do only under adult supervision.

14

© Carson-Dellosa CD-7322

## Heat Energy
# The Race is On

2 minutes

## What You Will Do

Show which molecules, cold or hot, move faster.

## Get it Together

- ◆ Two identical large, clear jars or glasses
- ◆ Food coloring (dark colors work best)
- ◆ Ice cold tap water
- ◆ Very hot tap water

## Procedure

1. Fill one jar with ice cold water and the other jar with very hot water.
2. Without moving the jars, place two drops of food coloring in each jar. Do not let the food coloring bottle touch the water.
3. Observe.

### A Closer Look

Warm water molecules move faster and are farther apart than cold water molecules. As the warm water molecules move quickly and spread, they take the food coloring with them.

**Attention!**
Avoid touching the hot water.

© Carson-Dellosa CD-7322

# Upward Flow

5 minutes

## What You Will Do

Demonstrate the upward flow of water.

## Get it Together

- 2 plastic soda bottles, 16 oz. or smaller
- Index card
- Bowl
- Food coloring
- Hot tap water
- Cold tap water

### A Closer Look

The colored water flows upward and starts to mix with the cold water above. Heating water makes it expand and get lighter. Since it is lighter, the water rises to the top and the heavier cold water begins to sink to the bottom. Swimmers notice that the water at the bottom of a pool, lake, or river is cooler than the water on the surface.

## Procedure

1. Carefully fill one bottle to the top with hot water.
2. Stand the bottle in the bowl and add a few drops of food coloring.
3. Quickly fill the other bottle with cold water.
4. Place the index card on top of the cold bottle.
5. Turn the bottle upside down, holding the card in place so the water will not leak out.
6. Stand it upside down on top of the colored hot water bottle. Make sure the top bottle balances on the bottom bottle.
7. Carefully pull out the card.

### Attention!
Use caution when working with hot water.

Cold

Hot

## What Now?

Try this again with the colored water in the top bottle and clear water in the bottom bottle.

16

© Carson-Dellosa CD-7322

# Compass Magnet

5 minutes

## What You Will Do

Demonstrate how to make a compass.

## Get it Together

- Cork
- Steel needle
- Magnet
- Bowl of water
- Tape

## Procedure

1. Magnetize the needle by rubbing the magnet on the needle in one direction about 20-25 times.
2. Tape the needle to the middle of the cork.
3. Place the cork in the water and observe.

### A Closer Look

When you magnetize the needle and allow it to move freely, it will point due north. This happens because a magnetized needle always aligns with the Earth's magnetic field.

**Attention!**
Use caution when working with the needle.

17

© Carson-Dellosa CD-7322

# I'm Attracted to You

2 minutes

## What You Will Do

Illustrate the use of a magnetic force.

## Get it Together

- 2-quart glass bowl
- Needle
- Thread
- Masking tape
- Bar magnet
- Water

## Procedure

1. Fill the bowl ³/₄ full with water.
2. Cut two 12" pieces of thread.
3. Tape both pieces of thread to one side of the bowl, about 1" apart.
4. Stretch the thread across the bowl and lay the needle across both pieces of thread.
5. Slowly lower the thread until the needle rests on the water's surface.
6. Gently move the thread out from under the needle. The needle should float on the surface of the water.
7. Move the magnet near, but do not touch the floating needle.

### A Closer Look

The needle floats on the surface of the water and moves when the magnet moves. The surface of the water acts like a thin skin. We call this surface tension. The needle is able to move across the surface of the water in response to the attractive forces of the magnet.

18

© Carson-Dellosa CD-7322

## Magnetism
# Pumped Up with Iron

2 minutes

## What You Will Do

Demonstrate a magnetic field.

## Get it Together

- ◆ Clean iron filings (science supply store)
- ◆ Bar magnets
- ◆ White sheet of paper
- ◆ Table

## Procedure

1. Place one bar magnet on the table.
2. Center the paper over the magnet.
3. Slowly sprinkle the iron filings over the length of the magnet.

### A Closer Look

A magnetic field is invisible, but it becomes observable when the iron filings are used to show the magnetic lines of force.

### Attention!

Do not get the iron filings in your eyes.

## What Now?

Use two bar magnets, one next to the other and repeat the procedure. Reverse the pole.

**19**

© Carson-Dellosa CD-7322

# Stacking Magnets

1 minute

## What You Will Do

Demonstrate how like magnetic poles repel each other.

## Get it Together

- ◆ Pencil
- ◆ 2 or more small, round, doughnut magnets that fit around the pencil

## Procedure

1. Place the magnets over the pencil.
2. Reverse the direction of the top magnet by flipping it over.

### A Closer Look

The magnets seem to float over each other because you have the like charges (+ and + or - and -) facing each other. The magnets will attract when you have opposite charges (+ and -) facing each other.

© Carson-Dellosa CD-7322

# Black and White

5 minutes

## What You Will Do

Demonstrate the reflective properties of light and dark colors.

## Get it Together

- 2 flashlights
- Two, 6" x 6" sheets of aluminum foil; one smooth, the other crumpled
- A sheet of white paper
- A sheet of black paper
- White shirt
- Black shirt
- Tape
- Dark room

### A Closer Look

The lighter colors reflect light back to your eyes while the darker colors absorb light. The same is true with the smooth foil. This illustrates why the safety tip of wearing lighter, reflective colors at night is important.

## Procedure

1. Tape the white paper to the wall, about 36" away. Tape the black paper to the wall.
2. Darken the room. Shine one flashlight on the white paper, and the other flashlight on the black paper. Note the difference in brightness.
3. Repeat Step 2 using the shirts. Observe which shirt is easier to see.
4. Repeat Step 2 using the aluminum foil. Note which one reflects the light to the ceiling.

© Carson-Dellosa CD-7322

# Bouncing Colors

2 minutes

## What You Will Do

Demonstrate the reflection and absorption of colors.

## Get it Together

◆ Flashlight
◆ Dark room
◆ Red sheet of cloth or paper
◆ One sheet each of red and blue colored cellophane

## Procedure

1. Darken the room and shine the flashlight on the red cloth or paper. It will look red.
2. Place the red cellophane over the flashlight and shine it at the red paper or cloth. It should still look red.
3. Remove the red cellophane and replace it with the blue sheet of cellophane. The red paper should look black.

### A Closer Look

When white light shines on red paper, the paper absorbs all of the colors except red, which it reflects back to your eyes. With the red cellophane, only red light gets through, which still gets reflected to your eyes. With the blue cellophane, red light gets absorbed and cannot be reflected, and that is why the paper looks black.

## What Now?

Try other combinations of colored cellophane.

© Carson-Dellosa CD-7322

# Bouncy, Bouncy

2 minutes

## What You Will Do

Visualize how light is reflected off a flat surface.

## Get it Together

◆ 2"-3" rubber ball
◆ A partner

## Procedure

1. Hold the ball in front of you.
2. Let it drop and notice it bounces straight up to your hand.
3. Facing your partner, stand a few feet away.
4. Bounce the ball to him. Notice the angle at which the ball hits.
5. Move back a few more feet from your partner and again bounce the ball to him. Notice the change in angle of the bounce.
6. Try bouncing the ball at a variety of angles.

### A Closer Look

You have created a model of how light bounces off a flat mirror, or reflector, at a particular angle. As the distance between you and your partner is greater, so is the angle of the bounce (or the angle of reflection).

© Carson-Dellosa CD-7322

# Can You Pour Me a Light?

3 minutes

## What You Will Do

Compare light reflection to fiber optics.

## Get it Together

- Tall, slim olive jar with lid
- Flashlight
- Nail
- Masking or plastic tape
- Newspaper
- Hammer
- Water
- Dark room
- Pan

### A Closer Look

Although light travels in straight lines, it is reflected at the water's surface and follows the path of the stream of water. Because of the bending, reflective properties of light, fiber optics can be used to direct light anywhere a wire can go, even into the veins and arteries of the human body.

## Procedure

1. With the hammer and nail, make two holes in the lid of the jar. Place the holes near the edge, but opposite each other. Work the nail in one of the holes to enlarge it a bit.
2. Fill the jar about ²/₃ with water, then place the lid on the jar.
3. Put tape over the holes.
4. Lay the jar and flashlight end to end, with the face of the flashlight at the bottom of the jar.
5. Roll the newspaper around the jar and flashlight to enclose them in a light-tube.
6. Darken the room and turn on the flashlight.
7. Hold the light-tube upright and remove the tape from the holes.
8. With the large nail hole down, pour the water into the pan.

### Attention!

Ask an adult for assistance when making the holes in the lid.

24

© Carson-Dellosa CD-7322

# Larger than Life

3 minutes

## What You Will Do

Demonstrate how a curved surface becomes a magnifier.

## Get it Together

- Sheet of newspaper
- 9" x 9" sheet of wax paper
- Eyedropper
- Water

## A Closer Look

You have made a magnifying "lens." The water drop is curved and see-through, and it bends the light as it travels from the page to your eye, making the print appear larger. The smaller the drop, the greater the curvature of the lens and the greater the magnification.

## Procedure

1. Place the wax paper on top of the newspaper.
2. With the eyedropper, place a small drop of water on the wax paper. Read the print.
3. Continue to make the drop bigger by adding more water.

© Carson-Dellosa CD-7322

# Mixing Colors

3 minutes

## What You Will Do

Demonstrate the mixing of the three primary colors.

## Get it Together

◆ Red, yellow, and blue food coloring
◆ Clear glass
◆ Water
◆ Spoon

## Procedure

1. Fill the glass with water.
2. Add two drops of red food coloring and stir.
3. Add two drops of yellow food coloring and stir.
4. Add two drops of blue food coloring and stir.

### A Closer Look

Your colors change from red to orange to purple. The secondary colors, orange and purple, are a combination of the primary colors, red, yellow, and blue.

### Attention!

Food coloring stains skin and clothing.

© Carson-Dellosa CD-7322

# Reversible Arrow

## What You Will Do

Demonstrate the bending of light rays.

## Get it Together

◆ 3" x 5" index card
◆ Marker or pen
◆ Clear jar or glass
◆ Water

## Procedure

1. Draw an arrow in the middle of the index card.
2. Fill the glass with water.
3. Place the card behind the glass.
4. Stand in front of the glass and slowly move the card away from it.

### A Closer Look

The arrow seems to reverse itself. This is because when light passes from one transparent material to another, for example, from water to air, it can change direction. This change in direction is called refraction, and it causes you to see the opposite of what is really there.

## What Now?

Use different shapes and objects behind the jar.

27

© Carson-Dellosa CD-7322

# The Missing Reflection

2 minutes

## What You Will Do

Compare light reflections of smooth and rough surfaces.

## Get it Together

◆ Sheet of smooth aluminum foil
◆ Sun or bright light

## Procedure

1. In the light, look at your reflection on the shiny side of the foil.
2. Crumple the foil into a loose wad.
3. Flatten out the wadded foil.
4. Again, look at your reflection.

### A Closer Look

When you looked at the smooth surface of the foil, the light rays were reflected in a straight line. When you crumpled the foil, the reflected light bounced off the rough surface in every direction, making it difficult to see your face.

28

© Carson-Dellosa CD-7322

# Vanishing Stamp

1 minute

## What You Will Do

Demonstrate the blocking of refracted rays.

## Get it Together

- ◆ Clear glass
- ◆ Water
- ◆ Postage stamp
- ◆ Saucer
- ◆ Table

## A Closer Look

The light rays bend as they pass at an angle from one medium to another. When you put the saucer on top of the glass, it screened off all the refracted light rays. Therefore, there was no angle from which the stamp could be seen.

## Procedure

1. Place the stamp picture-side up on a table.
2. Fill the glass with water and set it on top of the stamp.
3. Observe the stamp.
4. Place the saucer on top of the glass.
5. Again, observe the stamp.

29

© Carson-Dellosa CD-7322

# Water Magnifier

2 minutes

## What You Will Do

Show how water can magnify.

## Get it Together

◆ Paper clip
◆ Needle-nose pliers
◆ Cup of water
◆ Newspaper

## Procedure

1. Have an adult use the pliers to form a small loop in the end of the paper clip. Make the loop as round as possible.
2. Dip the loop in the water. A film of water should fill the loop.
3. Hold the loop above the newspaper and read.

### A Closer Look

The letters look larger because the surface tension causes the water to bend, creating a convex lens. This lens behaves the same as a magnifying glass by bending light rays that enter it.

### Attention!
Use caution when using pliers.

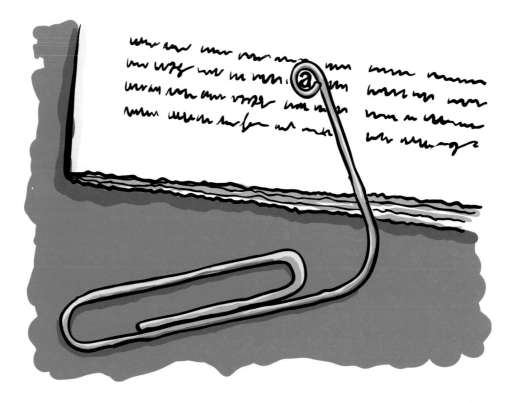

© Carson-Dellosa CD-7322

# Burning Up the Air

10 minutes

## What You Will Do

Demonstrate the reduction of air pressure through the burning of oxygen.

## Get it Together

- ◆ Clear, glass container
- ◆ Shallow pie tin
- ◆ Small candle
- ◆ Matches
- ◆ Water

## Procedure

1. Secure the candle in the middle of the pie tin. Do this by lighting the candle and dripping a few drops of wax on the tin, then placing the base of the candle on the hot wax. Allow it to dry for a few seconds.
2. Fill the pie tin to the top with water. Do not get the wick of the candle wet.
3. Light the candle.
4. Invert the glass and hold it over the candle for a minute.

### A Closer Look

The water in the glass rose higher than the original level of water in the pie pan. This happens because the flame consumed all the oxygen in the glass. The lost oxygen reduced the air pressure on the water, which allowed the water to rise up and take the place of the missing air in the glass.

### Attention!

Do this activity only under adult supervision. Use extreme caution when working with matches.

31

© Carson-Dellosa CD-7322

# Can Crush

5 minutes

## What You Will Do

Demonstrate the power of air pressure.

## Get it Together

◆ Burner, stove, or other heat source
◆ 1-gallon aluminum can with a screw top (hardware store)
◆ Oven mitt (to hold the hot can)
◆ ¹/₂ cup water

## Procedure

1. Make sure the can has been flushed out with water and is clean. Pour the water into the can. (Do not use a can that contained any type of dangerous chemical.)
2. Heat the can until you see a steady stream of steam being released. Allow the steam to be released for a couple of minutes.
3. Remove the can from the heat source.
4. Carefully, hold the can with your mitt and tightly place the screw top back on the can.
5. Stand back and observe.

### A Closer Look

During the heating process, the water evaporates and turns into a gas. The rising water vapor pushes much of the air out of the can. When the screw top is placed on the can, the air pressure outside the can is greater than the air pressure inside the can. To make the pressure inside and outside the can equal, the can tries to take up a smaller space, or implode. The same amount of air in a smaller space has a greater pressure, so it is more like the pressure outside the can.

### Attention!

Do this activity only under adult supervision. Use a mitt when handling the hot container. Keep all clothing away from the heat source.

32

© Carson-Dellosa CD-7322

Pressure
# Coin Sticks

1 minute

## What You Will Do

Prove the holding power of pressure.

## Get it Together

◆ Several different-sized coins
◆ A partner
◆ A few drops of water

## Procedure

1. Place a coin on your partner's forehead and press fairly hard (but not so hard that you hurt the person).
2. Place a few drops of water on the coin and repeat.
3. Repeat with different-sized coins.

### A Closer Look

When you press the coin on the forehead you are pushing out air and reducing air pressure. The pressure is slightly reduced causing a partial vacuum. This vacuum acts like a vacuum cleaner and holds the coin on the forehead. There is also some surface tension involved between the skin and coin.

33

© Carson-Dellosa CD-7322

# Dime's Worth

1 minute

## What You Will Do

Demonstrate a force called lift.

## Get it Together

◆ Dime or other small coin
◆ Smooth tabletop

## Procedure

1. Place the coin on the tabletop.
2. Keep your mouth level with the table and blow very hard over the top of the coin.

### A Closer Look

When you blow over the dime, you lower the air pressure above it. The air pressure above the dime is now less than the air pressure below. The unequal pressure on the dime creates a force called lift. Lift is what causes the coin to flip over. This is an example of Bernoulli's Principle. It states that when air moves faster over the top of an object than under its bottom, the greater pressure from underneath pushes the object upward. This force is what makes airplanes fly.

34

© Carson-Dellosa CD-7322

# Double Trouble

1 minute

## What You Will Do

Prove that air moves from an area of high pressure to an area of low pressure.

## Get it Together

- ◆ Glass
- ◆ Water
- ◆ Two identical drinking straws

## Procedure

1. Fill the glass with water.
2. Place both straws in your mouth.
3. Place the end of one straw in the glass of water and keep the other straw next to the glass in the open air.
4. Try drinking the water.

### A Closer Look

Normally when we inhale on a straw, our lungs expand. With the same amount of air in a larger space, the pressure inside our bodies is decreased and is less than the pressure outside our bodies. The higher pressure outside our bodies forces the water through the straw. When you add a second straw outside the glass, this pressure difference is not created, so no water comes through the straw.

35

© Carson-Dellosa CD-7322

# Funny Funnel

1 minute

## What You Will Do

Display how a change in air pressure can assist the movement of objects.

## Get it Together

- 3" x 5" index card
- Clean glass or plastic funnel, smaller than the index card
- Table or other flat surface

## Procedure

1. Place the index card on a table.
2. Place the wide end of the funnel over the card.
3. Inhale through the funnel.

### A Closer Look

Inhaling lowers the air pressure in the funnel. The normal air pressure in the room pushes the card toward the lower pressure that you create inside the funnel.

36

© Carson-Dellosa CD-7322

# Heart to Heart

2 minutes

## What You Will Do

Show how a change in air pressure can move objects.

## Get it Together

- Paper
- Pencil
- Tape
- Scissors

### A Closer Look

When you blow between the hearts, you lower the air pressure between them. The higher air pressure outside the hearts rushes into that empty space and pushes the hearts in with it, making them touch.

## Procedure

1. Cut a paper strip that it is 10" long x ½" wide.
2. Draw a heart at both ends of the strip.
3. Fold the paper strip in the middle and place it over the center of the pencil.
4. Tape the paper strip to the pencil.
5. Blow between the two hearts.

© Carson-Dellosa CD-7322

# Ice Cut

## What You Will Do

Illustrate the effect of pressure on ice.

## Get it Together

◆ Thin, metal wire about 16" long
◆ Bottle with a cork
◆ 2 heavy spoons or forks
◆ Ice cube
◆ Refrigerator

## Procedure

1. Push the cork into the bottle so that 1" sticks out from the top.
2. Tie the spoon or fork to each end of the wire.
3. Balance the ice cube on top of the cork.
4. Hang the wire over the ice cube.
5. Put the bottle in the refrigerator for several hours.

### A Closer Look

The pressure of the wire causes the ice below it to melt and the wire cuts easily through the cube. The water above the wire, no longer subject to the pressure, refreezes. This is the same process that takes place when people ice skate. The pressure from the weight of the blades melts the ice, allowing the skates to glide over water. When the pressure from the blade is gone, the water turns back into ice.

© Carson-Dellosa CD-7322

# It's All in the Cards

1 minute

## What You Will Do

Demonstrate lift in reverse.

## Get it Together

◆ Index card
◆ Table

## Procedure

1. Gently bend an index card widthwise and place it near the edge of the table.
2. Place your mouth even with the table.
3. Blow as hard as you can underneath the card.

### A Closer Look

The air stream from your breath lowers the air pressure underneath the card. Now the air pressure above the card is higher, so it creates a downward force. This force, another example of Bernoulli's Principle, causes the card to collapse and go flush with the table.

39

© Carson-Dellosa CD-7322

# It's Too Much Pressure

2 minutes

## What You Will Do

Demonstrate Pascal's Principle.

## Get it Together

♦ 2-liter plastic soda bottle with label removed
♦ Water

## Procedure

1. Fill the empty soda bottle to the top with water.
2. Screw the cap on tightly. There should be no bubbles in the bottle.
3. Lay the bottle on its side.
4. Pick a spot on the bottle, and push with your left thumb. Maintain a constant, firm pressure.
5. With your right thumb, push fairly hard on a spot on the other end of the bottle and notice what your left thumb feels.
6. Pick another spot on the bottle for your left thumb and repeat Step 5.

### A Closer Look

The water pressure increases when you push in the bottle with your right thumb. According to Pascal's Principle, when there is a change in pressure on a fluid in an enclosed space, that change is felt evenly throughout the fluid and by the walls of the container. You felt this principle as pressure under your left thumb.

© Carson-Dellosa CD-7322

**Pressure**

# Lemon Submarine

**5 minutes**

## What You Will Do

Demonstrate air compression.

## Get it Together

- Clean, glass jar
- Fresh lemon
- Large-sized balloon
- Scissors
- Rubber band
- Water

## Procedure

1. Cut a piece of lemon peel in the shape of a submarine.
2. Fill the jar to the top with water and put the lemon peel in it.
3. Cut a circle from the balloon and stretch it over the top of the jar.
4. Place the rubber band over the balloon to hold it in place.
5. While observing the submarine, press hard on the center of the balloon with your finger.
6. Remove your finger. Repeat.

### A Closer Look

Your submarine will sink when you push on the balloon and rise when you remove your finger. When you press on the balloon, you squash the small bubbles of air in the lemon peel into a smaller space, letting in extra water. This makes the lemon heavier, therefore, it will sink. When you take your finger away, the air pockets expand, pushing out excess water. This makes the lemon lighter and it will rise.

### Attention!
Use caution when working with the scissors.

41

© Carson-Dellosa CD-7322

Pressure
# Parachute

20 minutes

## What You Will Do

Illustrate how a large surface slows down a falling object.

## Get it Together

- ◆ 14" square cut from a plastic trash bag
- ◆ Four 14" lengths of string
- ◆ Small paper cup
- ◆ Hole punch

## Procedure

1. Poke a tiny hole in the center of the square.
2. Tie a knot in each corner of the square.
3. Tie a length of string above each knot.
4. Punch four holes evenly around the top of the cup.
5. Tie the loose ends of the string to each hole in the cup.
6. Toss your parachute high into the air and observe.
7. Stuff the parachute inside the cup and toss it into the air.

### A Closer Look

As the surface of the parachute spreads out, it encounters a great amount of air on its way down. This air offers resistance to the falling object and slows its fall to a gentle glide. When the parachute is stuffed inside the cup, the falling object is much smaller, and it encounters far less air to offer resistance. Therefore, it falls much faster.

42

© Carson-Dellosa CD-7322

# Rocket to the Moon

5 minutes

## What You Will Do

Observe the principles of rocket propulsion.

## Get it Together

- 15'-20' lightweight string or fishing line
- Several inches of cellophane tape
- Plastic drinking straw
- 6" balloon or larger
- 2 chairs

## Procedure

1. Thread the string through the straw.
2. Tie each end of the string to the backs of the chairs.
3. Move the chairs apart in a straight line until the string is taut.
4. Blow up the balloon.
5. Hold the balloon under the midpoint of the straw, so the opening faces the nearest chair. Do not allow air to escape.
6. Attach the tape over the middle of the straw so the balloon is secured.
7. Release the balloon and observe.

### A Closer Look

A rocket produces a pushing force, called thrust, to overcome gravity, which is the major obstacle for a rocket to get into space. Newton's Third Law of Motion states that for every action, there is an equal and opposite reaction. You supplied energy from your breath and trapped it in the balloon. When you released that energy under pressure, you drove your rocket into the set orbit (the string path).

43

© Carson-Dellosa CD-7322

**Pressure**

# Sticky Plates

1 minute

## What You Will Do

Illustrate how a vacuum affects air pressure.

## Get it Together

- ◆ 2 dinner plates (about 8" or 9")
- ◆ Pan of water
- ◆ Level surface

## Procedure

1. Stack the two plates on a level surface. Lift the top plate by its rim and replace.
2. Submerge the stacked plates in the pan of water until they settle at the bottom.
3. Pick up the plates from the bottom (do not shake off the excess water) and place them on the level surface.
4. Try to lift the top plate by its rim.

### A Closer Look

The water creates a seal which makes the top plate stick to the bottom plate. When the plates were dry, the air pressure was equal on all sides, and the top plate lifted off easily. As water displaced the air, it formed a partial vacuum (a lack of air), which acted like a plunger, and held the plates together.

© Carson-Dellosa CD-7322

# The Final Straw

1 minute

## What You Will Do

Demonstrate how a perfume sprayer works.

## Get it Together

◆ Drinking straw
◆ Glass of water
◆ Scissors

## Procedure

1. Make a cut in the middle of the straw that goes ¾ through it.
2. Place the straw in the water so that the cut is above the water's surface.
3. Hold and bend the top half of the straw parallel to the bottom of the glass.
4. Blow hard through the horizontal part of the straw.

### A Closer Look

As you blew across the top of the lower section of straw, you decreaed the air pressure inside that section of straw. The higher pressure in the room pushes down on the water in the glass, forcing a mist of liquid up through the straw. Squeezing a perfume sprayer produces the same effect.

© Carson-Dellosa CD-7322

# Two Holes Are Better

1 minute

## What You Will Do

Prove that liquids can flow faster and more evenly with balanced air pressure.

## Get it Together

◆ Unopened juice can
◆ Manual punch can opener or awl
◆ Bowl or pitcher

## Procedure

1. Punch a small hole in the top edge of the can.
2. Pour some juice in the bowl.
3. Punch a second hole near the opposite edge of the can.
4. Pour the remainder of the juice in the bowl.

### A Closer Look

As the juice leaves the can, it must be replaced with air. With only one hole, the juice and the air compete for the same opening. That is why the flow of juice is gurgled and interrupted. When you add a second hole, juice flows out one hole while air flows into the other. This balance of pressure allows the juice to flow freely.

46

© Carson-Dellosa CD-7322

# Do My Ears Deceive Me?

2 minutes

## What You Will Do

Illustrate the Doppler effect.

## Get it Together

◆ Foam ball (any type)
◆ 9-volt battery
◆ Piezo buzzer attached to 9-volt battery clips (Electronics store)
◆ Knife
◆ A partner

## Procedure

1. Have an adult carefully slit an opening in the center of the ball with the knife, about ¹/₂ the thickness of the ball.
2. Attach the battery clips to the 9-volt battery.
3. Gently embed the Piezo buzzer with battery clips and the 9-volt battery in the ball.
4. Play catch with the buzzing ball across the room, being attentive to how the buzzer sounds as it moves toward you and away from you.

### A Closer Look

The pitch of the buzzer should become higher as the ball moves toward you and lower as the ball moves away from you. This is known as the Doppler effect. The Doppler effect occurs whenever there is a source of moving sound (like the buzzing ball or an ambulance siren). As the ball gets closer, a larger number of shorter sound waves reach your ear. Your ear interprets this as a higher pitch. As the ball gets farther away, the same number of sound waves take a longer time to reach your ear and they spread out, or get longer, as they travel. You perceive the less-frequent, longer sound waves as a decreased pitch.

### Attention!
Use caution when cutting the ball with the knife.

## What Now?

Listen carefully as you try running toward or away from the stationary, buzzing ball. Also, run along side the buzzing ball tossed by your partner.

© Carson-Dellosa CD-7322

# Krazy Kazoo

5 minutes

## What You Will Do

Explore sound vibration.

## Get it Together

- ◆ Scissors
- ◆ Empty cardboard tube from a paper towel roll
- ◆ Wax paper
- ◆ Rubber band

### A Closer Look

The sound waves from your voice traveled through the tube, reached the wax paper, and made the wax paper vibrate. This vibration amplified and changed the way your voice sounds. The hole was needed in the tube so air could enter the tube.

## Procedure

1. Cut a dime-sized hole in the middle of the cardboard tube.
2. Cut a 4" x 4" piece of wax paper.
3. Stretch the wax paper tightly over one end of the tube.
4. Fasten the paper to the tube with the rubber band.
5. Place the tube in your mouth and hum.

## What Now?

Try different tube lengths, different types of papers, or different-sized air holes.

© Carson-Dellosa CD-7322

# Water Trombone

3 minutes

## What You Will Do

Make a simple musical instrument.

## Get it Together

- Drinking straw
- Water
- Soda bottle

## Procedure

1. Pour water into the bottle until it is about ³/₄ full.
2. Put the straw in the bottle.
3. Blow across the top of the straw using a steady exhale.
4. Lift the straw and continue to blow.

## A Closer Look

Different sounds were heard as the straw was lifted. As the straw is lowered, the sound gets higher in pitch. As the straw is raised, the pitch gets lower. The lengthening and lowering of the column of air in the straw is the basic way a slide trombone works.

© Carson-Dellosa CD-7322

# Homemade Electroscope

5 minutes

## What You Will Do

Observe static electricity through the use of an electroscope.

## Get it Together

- Aluminum foil
- 10"-12" of string
- Plastic foam ball
- Piece of wool cloth

- Plastic comb
- Table
- Tape

## Procedure

1. Cover the ball with aluminum foil.
2. Tape one end of the string to the foil-covered ball.
3. Tape the other end of the string to the edge of a table so the ball can swing freely.
4. With the wool, rub the comb several times.
5. Touch the charged comb to the ball. Observe.
6. Touch the ball to the ground. This is called grounding.

Note: This activity works best when the relative humidity in the air is under 50%.

### A Closer Look

The comb is attracted to your homemade electroscope. An electroscope is a scientific instrument used to detect electrical charge or static electricity. Negatively charged particles called electrons, which are on the comb, are attracted to the foil, which has a positive charge. Because positive and negative charges are attracted to each other, the electroscope moves toward the comb. When you touched the ball to the ground, you removed the charges.

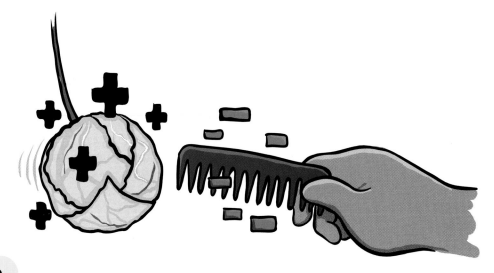

## What Now?

Try charging other objects to your electroscope, such as a balloon, a pen, and metal objects.

50

© Carson-Dellosa CD-7322

# I Have a Leg Up on You

3 minutes

## What You Will Do

Demonstrate static electricity.

## Get it Together

◆ Sheer nylon stocking washed in clear water
◆ Clear, lightweight plastic bag
◆ Smooth wall

## Procedure

1. Holding the stocking at the top, place it flush against the wall.
2. Rub the plastic bag on the stocking about 20 times, using long strokes in one direction.
3. Release your hold on the stocking.

Note: This activity works best when the relative humidity in the air is under 50%.

## A Closer Look

The nylon stocking should cling to the wall. As the plastic is rubbed on the nylon, it will remove the negative charge and give the nylon a positive charge. The positively-charged nylon will stick to the wall because the wall has a negative charge. Opposite charges are attracted to each other.

© Carson-Dellosa CD-7322

Static Electricity
# I'm Stuck on You

1 minute

## What You Will Do

Demonstrate the effects of static electricity.

## Get it Together

◆ Cellophane tape
◆ Table

## Procedure

1. Cut two 6" pieces of tape and press them on the table, leaving a small piece hanging over the edge.
2. Grasp both the ends of the tape, one in each hand, and quickly pull both pieces off the table.
3. Bring the two pieces near each other, but do not allow them to touch.

### A Closer Look

The pieces of tape moved away from each other because all materials are made of atoms, which have positive and negative charges. When there is a gain or loss of charges, the object is said to have static electricity. Pulling the tape causes it to pick up negatively-charged electrons from the table. Since both pieces of tape have a like charge, they repel, or push away from each other.

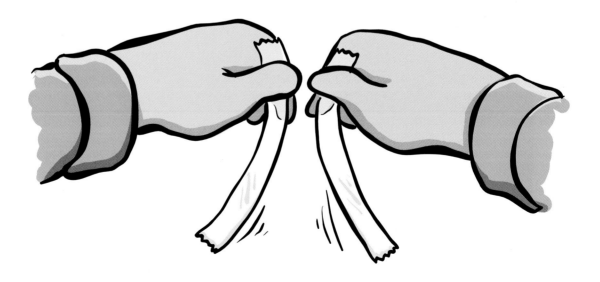

© Carson-Dellosa CD-7322

# The Magic Toothpick

5 minutes

## What You Will Do

Use a magic trick to prove the existence of static electricity.

## Get it Together

- Flat toothpick
- Nickel or other smooth-edged coin that will stand on its side
- Balloon
- Clear, plastic cup

## A Closer Look

The toothpick moves as you move the balloon around it. Rubbing a balloon on your hair causes it to become negatively charged. The attractive force between the negatively charged balloon and the positively charged toothpick is strong enough to cause the movement.

## Procedure

1. Stand the coin on its edge.
2. Balance the toothpick across the top of the coin.
3. Carefully cover the coin and toothpick with the cup. Do not allow the toothpick to touch the cup.
4. Blow up the balloon and "charge" it by rubbing it against your hair or a sweater several times.
5. Slowly move the balloon around the cup and observe.

Note: This activity works best when the relative humidity of the air is under 50%.

© Carson-Dellosa CD-7322

# Tug of War

**3 minutes**

## What You Will Do

Demonstrate the difference in pulling power between water and alcohol.

## Get it Together

- 12" aluminum foil
- Red or blue food coloring
- Rubbing alcohol
- Eye dropper
- Water
- Measuring cup

## Procedure

1. Add a few drops of food coloring to ½ cup of water.
2. Smooth the sheet of aluminum foil on a flat surface.
3. Pour an extremely thin layer of the colored water onto the foil.
4. Using the eyedropper, add one drop of alcohol to the center of the colored water.

### A Closer Look

The instant separation between the water and the alcohol is because of a property called cohesion. Cohesion is the tendency of like molecules to want to stick together; they resist being pulled apart. However, after the alcohol has a chance to settle, the positive and negative charges of both water and alcohol mingle, and the two liquids mix.

© Carson-Dellosa CD-7322

## Static Electricity
# Unpeppering the Salt

2 minutes

## What You Will Do

Display how static electricity can attract lightweight objects.

## Get it Together

- 1 Tbsp. pepper
- 1 Tbsp. salt
- Rubber or plastic comb
- Paper

### A Closer Look

The lightweight pepper has a positive charge and it is attracted to the negatively charged comb. The salt is heavier and the force of static electricity is not enough to propel it upward.

## Procedure

1. Mix the salt and pepper together on a piece of paper.
2. Comb your hair 25 to 30 times — quickly, (long, smooth hair or curly, unruly hair works best).
3. Hold the comb over the salt and pepper mixture and observe.

Note: This activity works best when the relative humidity of the air is under 50%.

## What Now?

Try this activity with a brush. Also try to pick up other small items, such as bits of paper, other flakes of spices, etc.

© Carson-Dellosa CD-7322

# Floating Needle

5 minutes

## What You Will Do

Compare the effects of surface tension and density on a metal object.

## Get it Together

- ◆ Clear, plastic cup
- ◆ Small sewing needle
- ◆ Rectangular-shaped piece of paper to fit inside the cup
- ◆ Vegetable oil
- ◆ Water

## Procedure

1. Fill the cup about ¾ full with water.
2. Carefully place the paper on top of the water so it floats.
3. Dip the needle in the oil.
4. Quickly and gently set the needle on top of the floating paper.
5. Observe what happens as the paper sinks into the water.

### A Closer Look

The needle maintains its floating position even after the paper sinks. This is because water molecules like to stick together with a strong force called surface tension. The coating of oil on the needle helps maintain surface tension because oil and water do not mix.

### Attention!
The needle is sharp. Use caution.

## What Now?

Try different types of oils and different-sized needles.

© Carson-Dellosa CD-7322

# Geo-panes

30 minutes

## What You Will Do

Experiment with the low surface tension of bubbles.

## Get it Together

- ◆ Box of toothpicks
- ◆ Lump of clay
- ◆ Thread
- ◆ Liquid dish soap
- ◆ Large bucket
- ◆ Water
- ◆ Glycerin, optional (drug store)

## Procedure

1. Build numerous geometric shapes (square, rectangle, triangle, etc.) from the toothpicks. This can be done by connecting the edges of the toothpicks with small pea-sized balls of clay.
2. Tie a 6" piece of thread to each figure.
3. Fill the bucket with 6" of water and add a couple of big squirts of dish soap to the water. For better bubbles, add a couple of spoonfuls of clear glycerin.
4. Dip your shapes into the soapy water.
5. Blow gently into the film to create bubbles.

### A Closer Look

Soapy film fills the insides of the toothpicks. If you blow on this film, you will make bubbles. Detergent reduces the surface tension of water and substances with a low surface tension have a tendency to form films. When you blow on the bubbles they behave like elastic membranes until they reach the limits of stretchability and pop.

**Attention!**
Avoid getting soap in your eyes.

## Clean Up

Flush used solution down the drain with plenty of water.

© Carson-Dellosa CD-7322

# Half Full or Half Empty?

5 minutes

## What You Will Do

Demonstrate a relationship between surface tension and air pressure.

## Get it Together

◆ 2 identical drinking glasses
◆ Bowl
◆ Drinking straw
◆ Sink
◆ Water

### A Closer Look

Air pressure outside the glass combines with surface tension to keep water in the top glass from leaking out when the rims are separated. When you blow into the straw, you change the air pressure and overcome the water's surface tension.

## Procedure

1. Fill the sink with water so it is higher than the width of the glasses.
2. Fill the glasses with water by placing them in the sink.
3. Press the rims of the glasses together underwater.
4. Carefully remove the glasses from the sink with the rims held together and set them in the bowl so one glass is exactly on top of the other.
5. Slowly, and carefully, slide the top glass slightly to one side so the rims no longer meet. If done slowly, no water should leak out.
6. Aim the straw at the point where there is space between the two glasses and blow.

58

© Carson-Dellosa CD-7322

# Jumping Wire

10 minutes

## What You Will Do

Demonstrate the force of surface tension.

## Get it Together

- Liquid dish soap
- Bowl
- Bendable metal wire, plus a straight piece of wire
- Glycerin, optional (drug store)
- Water

### A Closer Look

When you pop one side of the bubble, the wire is pulled in by surface tension, decreasing the size of the bubble. This causes the wire to jump from the frame.

## Procedure

1. Place a few ounces of liquid soap in the bowl and add water. For a stronger bubble solution, add a tablespoon of glycerin.
2. Bend the wire to form a rectangular frame and handle.
3. Dip the wire into the soap solution.
4. Hold your "wand" level with the soap and place the straight piece of wire across the center of it.
5. Carefully break the soap film on one side of the wire with your finger and observe.

## What Now?

Tie a short piece of thread inside the wire frame. The thread should be shorter than the inside of the rectangular frame. Dip the frame in the soap and break the film inside the loop.

59

© Carson-Dellosa CD-7322

# Row, Row, Row Your Boat

3 minutes

## What You Will Do

Investigate how changes in surface tension cause movement.

## Get it Together

- Index card
- Scissors
- Rectangular pan
- Liquid dish soap

## A Closer Look

Your boat can float on top of the water because of surface tension. Changes in surface tension can actually cause fluid to flow. When you place a drop of detergent at the back of your boat, the surface tension is broken and your boat is propelled forward.

## Procedure

1. Cut a little boat shape from the index card. Make sure to put a small rectangular notch in the back and a point in the front.
2. Fill the pan with water and gently place the boat in the pan.
3. Place a drop of soap in the notch of the boat.
4. To repeat the activity you must wash the pan after each trial.

## What Now?

Try other shapes and sizes for your boat and race with a partner.

© Carson-Dellosa CD-7322

# Sugar and Spice

2 minutes

## What You Will Do

Demonstrate the concept of surface tension.

## Get it Together

- ◆ Bowl of water
- ◆ Pepper shaker
- ◆ Spoon
- ◆ Bar of soap
- ◆ 1 tsp. sugar

### A Closer Look

Surface tension allows the pepper to float on the water. The bar of soap breaks this tension and the pepper floats away from that spot. The sugar pushes the soap film under its crystals, allowing the surface tension to reform. The pepper then floats back to the center.

## Procedure

1. Shake the pepper into the bowl of water in a thin, even layer.
2. Dip the soap in the center of the pepper for a minute. Observe the pepper moving away from the soap.
3. Slowly sprinkle the sugar onto the water where the soap was. Observe the pepper as it returns to its original position.

61

© Carson-Dellosa CD-7322

# The Wet Nickel

5 minutes

## What You Will Do

Illustrate how water molecules have a strong attractive force.

## Get it Together

◆ Eyedropper
◆ Nickel or other similarly-sized coin
◆ Paper towel
◆ 1 cup water

## Procedure

1. Place the coin on the paper towel.
2. Using the eyedropper, slowly place drops of water on the coin, one at a time.
3. Count the drops until the water flows over the sides of the coin.

### A Closer Look

If you used a nickel, It should take about 50 to 70 drops of water before the water dome breaks. If you used another coin, your results may vary. The water adheres to the surface of the coin because of surface tension. When the weight of water was too great for the surface tension to hold, the water overflowed.

62

© Carson-Dellosa CD-7322

# Walking Water

5 minutes

## What You Will Do

Exhibit how water can travel on a straight surface without falling off.

## Get it Together

- ◆ 12" string (not thread)
- ◆ Small nail
- ◆ Pot or pail (to catch the pouring water)
- ◆ Plastic cup
- ◆ Water

## A Closer Look

Gravity causes the water to travel down the string until it reaches your right finger and the pail. The molecules near the surface of the water cling together to form an elastic tube-like skin through which the water flows. The elastic skin is also known as surface tension.

## Procedure

1. Punch a small hole near the top of the plastic cup with the nail.
2. Dampen the string and place it through the hole, tying a knot from the inside.
3. Fill the cup almost to the top with water.
4. Place the pail on a waist-high surface.
5. Tie the free end of the string to your right index finger and hold it over the pail.
6. Hold the cup in your left hand.
7. Stretch the string taut and slant it downward toward the pail.
8. Tip the cup of water and slowly pour the water onto the string and into the pail.

63

© Carson-Dellosa CD-7322

# Water Blockade

2 minutes

## What You Will Do

Demonstrate how surface tension prevents water leakage.

## Get it Together

◆ Glass bottle with a narrow mouth
◆ First-aid gauze
◆ Rubber band

## Procedure

1. Fill the bottle to the top with water.
2. Place the gauze over the mouth of the bottle.
3. Secure the gauze with the rubber band.
4. Turn the bottle upside down.
5. Touch the gauze with your finger.

### A Closer Look

Water likes to stick together in drops of a certain size. When the holes of the gauze are very small, surface tension prevents drops from forming and slipping through. When you press on the gauze, you stretch those holes and make them large enough for water drops to form and fall through.

64

© Carson-Dellosa CD-7322